Benjamin Banneker

American Mathematician and Astronomer

Colonial Leaders

Lord Baltimore
English Politician and Colonist

Benjamin Banneker
American Mathematician and Astronomer

Sir William Berkeley
Governor of Virginia

William Bradford
Governor of Plymouth Colony

Jonathan Edwards
Colonial Religious Leader

Benjamin Franklin
American Statesman, Scientist, and Writer

Anne Hutchinson
Religious Leader

Cotton Mather
Author, Clergyman, and Scholar

Increase Mather
Clergyman and Scholar

James Oglethorpe
Humanitarian and Soldier

William Penn
Founder of Democracy

Sir Walter Raleigh
English Explorer and Author

Caesar Rodney
American Patriot

John Smith
English Explorer and Colonist

Miles Standish
Plymouth Colony Leader

Peter Stuyvesant
Dutch Military Leader

George Whitefield
Clergyman and Scholar

Roger Williams
Founder of Rhode Island

John Winthrop
Politician and Statesman

John Peter Zenger
Free Press Advocate

Revolutionary War Leaders

John Adams
Second U.S. President

Samuel Adams
Patriot

Ethan Allen
Revolutionary Hero

Benedict Arnold
Traitor to the Cause

John Burgoyne
British General

George Rogers Clark
American General

Lord Cornwallis
British General

Thomas Gage
British General

King George III
English Monarch

Nathanael Greene
Military Leader

Nathan Hale
Revolutionary Hero

Alexander Hamilton
First U.S. Secretary of the Treasury

John Hancock
President of the Continental Congress

Patrick Henry
American Statesman and Speaker

William Howe
British General

John Jay
First Chief Justice of the Supreme Court

Thomas Jefferson
Author of the Declaration of Independence

John Paul Jones
Father of the U.S. Navy

Thaddeus Kosciuszko
Polish General and Patriot

Lafayette
French Freedom Fighter

James Madison
Father of the Constitution

Francis Marion
The Swamp Fox

James Monroe
American Statesman

Thomas Paine
Political Writer

Molly Pitcher
Heroine

Paul Revere
American Patriot

Betsy Ross
American Patriot

Baron Von Steuben
American General

George Washington
First U.S. President

Anthony Wayne
American General

Famous Figures of the Civil War Era

John Brown
Abolitionist

Jefferson Davis
Confederate President

Frederick Douglass
Abolitionist and Author

Stephen A. Douglas
Champion of the Union

David Farragut
Union Admiral

Ulysses S. Grant
Military Leader and President

Stonewall Jackson
Confederate General

Joseph E. Johnston
Confederate General

Robert E. Lee
Confederate General

Abraham Lincoln
Civil War President

George Gordon Meade
Union General

George McClellan
Union General

William Henry Seward
Senator and Statesman

Philip Sheridan
Union General

William Sherman
Union General

Edwin Stanton
Secretary of War

Harriet Beecher Stowe
Author of Uncle Tom's Cabin

James Ewell Brown Stuart
Confederate General

Sojourner Truth
Abolitionist, Suffragist, and Preacher

Harriet Tubman
Leader of the Underground Railroad

Colonial Leaders

Benjamin Banneker

American Mathematician and Astronomer

Bonnie Hinman

Arthur M. Schlesinger, jr.
Senior Consulting Editor

Chelsea House Publishers

Philadelphia

Produced by Robert Gerson Publisher's Services, Avondale, PA

CHELSEA HOUSE PUBLISHERS
Editor in Chief Stephen Reginald
Production Manager Pamela Loos
Director of Photography Judy L. Hasday
Art Director Sara Davis
Managing Editor James D. Gallagher

Staff for *BENJAMIN BANNEKER*
Project Editor Anne Hill
Project Editor/Publishing Coordinator Jim McAvoy
Contributing Editor Amy Handy
Associate Art Director Takeshi Takahashi
Series Design Keith Trego

The Chelsea House World Wide Web address is http://www.chelseahouse.com

5 7 9 8 6

Library of Congress Cataloging-in-Publication Data

Hinman, Bonnie.
Benjamin Banneker / by Bonnie Hinman
    p. cm. — (Colonial leaders)
Includes bibliographical references and index.
Summary: A biography of the eighteenth–century African American
who taught himself mathematics and astronomy and helped survey what
would become Washington, D.C.
ISBN 0-7910-5348-2 (hc); 0-7910-5691-0 (pb)
1. Banneker, Benjamin, 1731–1806 Juvenile literature.
2. Astronomers—United States Biography Juvenile literature.
3. Afro–American scientists—United States Biography Juvenile
literature. [1. Banneker, Benjamin, 1731–1806. 2. Astronomers.
3. Afro–Americans Biography.] I. Title. II. Series.
QB36.B22H56   1999
520' .92—dc21
[B]   99-24118
                                                                    CIP

Contents

In the 1700s, during Benjamin Banneker's time, tobacco was an important crop grown on many farms, including the one owned by the Banneker family. Their farm probably looked much like this one.

The Tobacco Farmer's Son

Wildcats and wolves and a few bears hid in the nearby woods when Benjamin Banneker was born. It was November 9, 1731. The new baby slept peacefully in the sturdy log cabin where he lived with his family. The Banneker family lived in Maryland. It was still an English colony in 1731. Thirteen colonies made up the new land of America. They weren't states yet because the king of England was the ruler.

Baby Ben didn't care about a king who lived far away across the ocean. He was happy to live with his parents and grandmother and aunts on their tobacco farm. Everyone worked hard to grow the tobacco plants. At first Ben played in the dirt and grass as the others worked. But soon he learned to pick bugs from the tobacco leaves. It was an important job because too many bugs might destroy the tobacco crop.

Many farmers in Maryland grew tobacco. The weather and soil were just right. The Bannekers and their neighbors could make a good living raising tobacco.

Young Ben and his parents were free blacks. Most black men and women were slaves during Ben's lifetime. But Ben's mother, Mary, was never a slave. Ben's father, Robert, had been freed as a young man. That meant that Ben was free, too.

Ben's grandmother, Molly Welsh, was different from the rest of his family. She was white. Ben loved to listen to his grandmother tell the exciting story of how she came to America many years before.

Young Molly had worked for a farmer in England. She helped take care of his cows. One day a cow kicked over the milk bucket while

Molly was milking. The milk spilled on the barn floor. The farmer said Molly stole the milk, and he had her arrested.

The laws in England then were very strict. Stealing was one of 300 crimes that could be punished by death.

In court the judge asked Molly if she could read. Ben's grandmother proudly said yes. The judge banged his gavel and said she would be sent to America as her punishment. One of the rules said a person who could read might be sent there as a worker. Molly was saved!

She arrived in Maryland about 1683. For seven years Molly worked on a big tobacco plantation. She was an **indentured servant.** An indentured servant worked without pay for a certain number of years to pay back the plantation owner. The owner had paid for the servant's boat trip from England. It was a lot like being a slave, but an indentured servant was free to leave when the time was over. Most servants worked for five or seven years.

At last Molly was free, but she didn't have any place to go or any money. Ben's grandmother didn't let that stop her. She rented a piece of land and grew her own tobacco. After a few years she saved enough money to buy a small patch of land. Several years later she purchased two slaves.

His grandmother often told Ben that she didn't like slavery. After being an indentured servant, Molly knew that slavery was wrong. But she needed help on her tobacco farm. She felt buying slaves was the only way to get that help.

One of the slaves was strong and healthy and a good worker. He helped Molly cut down trees to clear more land. He helped her take care of the farm animals and plant more tobacco.

The other slave was different. He wasn't as strong or as willing to work. In fact he didn't like to do the hard farm work at all. But Ben's grandmother liked his quiet dignified ways. She gave him easy chores. Day by day they learned how to talk to each other.

TO BE SOLD, on board the Ship *Bance-Ifland*, on tuefday the 6th of *May* next, at *Afbley-Ferry*; a choice cargo of about 250 fine healthy NEGROES, juft arrived from the Windward & Rice Coaft. ⸻The utmoft care has already been taken, and fhall be continued, to keep them free from the leaft danger of being infected with the SMALL-POX, no boat having been on board, and all other communication with people from *Charles-Town* prevented.

Auftin, Laurens, & Appleby.

N. B. Full one Half of the above Negroes have had the SMALL-POX in their own Country.

Notices such as this one appeared in colonial newspapers to advertise that slaves were available for sale.

The slave called himself Bannaka. He claimed to be an African prince. His father, the chief of their people, had enemies. These enemies sold Bannaka to the slave traders. The traders brought him to America on a crowded slave ship.

In a few years Molly set her slaves free. Soon after that she married Bannaka. He was Ben's grandfather. He had died many years before Ben was born, but Ben's grandmother's eyes still lit up with pleasure when she told the story of the African prince.

Ben's father and grandfather came to America from Africa in slave ships. Slaves were locked below the ship's deck in holds. Each person might have a space to sit or lie that was only 18 inches wide. Many Africans died before reaching America. Some jumped overboard to escape the horrible conditions.

As Ben grew older, there was less time for stories and more time for work. He helped his father take care of the cows and feed the chickens. Together they pulled weeds from around the tiny tobacco plants. Ben's father was a good farmer. But the farm belonged to Ben's grandmother. Ben's parents wanted to own their own farm. After several years of hard work, they saved enough money to buy some land.

Ben was six years old when he moved with his parents and little sisters to their new home. Ben's name was written on the land **deed** right

A farm requires a lot of land and hard work. The crops and the animals have to be tended to everyday. Young Ben helped out with both.

after his father's. Ben's father knew how important it was to own land. He wanted to be sure that the land would always belong to Ben.

During this time Ben's grandmother had been teaching him to read. Her only book was a big Bible she had ordered from England. Soon Ben could read many words from the Bible. When the reading lesson was done, she taught him to count. Ben loved numbers. He counted bugs and trees and birds and anything else he saw around him.

One day his grandmother said Ben needed to go to school. She said a boy who was so quick to learn must go to a real school. She arranged for Ben to attend a one-room school that had recently opened nearby. When school started, Ben put on a new shirt, waved to his grandmother, and walked to school with his mother.

White students and a few other free black students like Ben attended the school. Ben's teacher was surprised that he could read so many words. Ben loved school. He had many

Unlike today's schools with their many class-rooms, schools in Ben's time usually had just one room and one teacher.

books to read instead of just his grandmother's Bible. When he wasn't reading, Ben made up math problems and puzzles.

Ben's school was only open a few months each year. Students had to help with farm work in the spring and summer. Ben looked forward to the first day of school late in the fall.

Reading and writing and math were most important to Ben, but he also found a new friend. Jacob Hall, another free black, was Ben's classmate. Jacob and Ben were friends for their whole lives.

During the long days of summer, Ben sometimes walked through the woods and fields nearby. Next to reading and counting, walking outside was his favorite thing to do. He liked to watch and listen to the Patapsco River. It roared through a rocky bed less than a mile from Ben's home.

As each year went by, Ben had to spend more time working on the farm and less time at school. Finally his school days ended. Most boys his age were glad to be done with school but not Ben. He was sad. But young Ben was a Banneker, and Bannekers made the best of things. When he wasn't milking the cows or cutting tobacco or cleaning out the barn, Ben was studying. He borrowed books that he read in his free time. Sometimes he made up math word puzzles to ask his family or neighbors. Ben wanted to learn about everything.

Ben's early years were full of hard work, but he was happy. His family loved and encouraged him even when they didn't understand some of the subjects he liked to study.

When Ben was around 20 years old, he did something that made people take notice of him. It was probably the first time that anyone outside of his family paid much attention to Benjamin Banneker, but it wouldn't be the last time.

Ben was determined to make a clock, but first he had to study how the pieces should go together. So he borrowed a watch to take apart, in order to learn all about the complex inner workings of a timepiece.

The Wooden Clock

Ben decided to make a clock. A clock or watch was rarely seen in the 1700s in America. In cities the churches might ring their bells at certain times of the day. But most farmers lived too far from churches to hear their bells. In Ben's valley a cannon fired to signal important events. The boom of the cannon usually meant that a ship had arrived at a nearby plantation **wharf**. It might be a supply ship or a slave ship. If the farmers needed to shop, they went to the river.

The colonists had little need to know the exact time. Farmers like Ben and his family began their workday when the sun came up, ate a meal when the sun was high overhead, and quit working when the sun went down.

He may not have needed a clock, but Ben wanted to make one. The many pieces of a clock had to fit together just right before the clock would run. Perhaps it was just one more math puzzle to Ben.

The young tobacco farmer faced one big problem. He had never seen the inside of a clock or even a watch. How could Ben make something without seeing it first? That problem was solved when someone loaned him a pocket watch.

Soon Ben had taken the watch apart to study the gears and wheels. He looked at each piece and drew many pictures of what he saw. The tiny wheels inside the pocket watch fit together perfectly. Ben had to figure out how to make the parts bigger for the clock he planned. For this he used the math skills that he had studied and practiced for so long.

At last he began to carve. Most of Ben's clock was made from wood. Sometimes he had to

Carving each piece carefully by hand, Ben
made his clock out of wood. This clock dates
from a few years later but is similar to the one
Ben constructed.

throw a part away and start over. One by one the wheels and gears were done. Ben worked on the clock in his spare time just as he had studied when he was younger.

It took more than a year for Ben to finish his clock. When it was done, he added a bell that rang on the hour.

Ben's neighbors soon heard about his accomplishment. They were amazed. Not only did the clock run, but it kept **accurate** time. Visitors soon arrived at the Banneker farm to see the wondrous wooden clock. People who lived in the valley had never heard of Benjamin Banneker the farmer. Now they talked about Benjamin Banneker the clockmaker.

Ben liked to show the clock to visitors, but he spent most of his time working on the farm. Tobacco plants needed a lot of attention. Small flies and beetles liked to eat the seedlings. Later, tobacco caterpillars wanted to chew on the full-grown plants. In August the plants had to be cut and prepared for sale. The leaves had to hang in a

After all the work of raising the tobacco plants, they had to be harvested and hung in a barn or tobacco house to dry out.

tobacco house for several weeks before they were ready to be packed and sold. Then it was time to clear more land for planting the next spring.

A few years after Ben finished the clock, his father died. Now Ben was in charge. He lived on the farm with his mother, Mary. His sisters married and moved to their own homes nearby.

Ben was a good farmer just like his father. He grew a large vegetable garden besides the tobacco. He tended several beehives that his father had started. The barn held a couple of cows and horses, and chickens scratched in the barnyard dirt. Ben worked hard all day long.

Ben still found time to read. At first he read borrowed books. But in 1763 he bought his first book. It was a Bible, and he purchased it from a neighbor. He was excited to own a book of his own at last.

In the front of the Bible he wrote, "I bought this book of Honora Buchanan the 4th day of January 1763. B.B." He also wrote his birthdate and the date of his father's death. Ben kept the Bible his whole life.

Benjamin also owned a flute and a violin. He never said later in his life when or where he got the instruments. He may have bought them from one of the supply ships. Somehow he learned to play both of them. At the end of a long day of work, he often sat on his porch and played songs. Sometimes his family sang along.

Ben led a quiet life on the farm. He may have felt lonely sometimes, but he never complained. It wasn't easy for free blacks to fit in with the other farmers in the valley. Many people didn't think free blacks should be equal to whites. Yet they respected Ben for his skills in math and farming. Often they asked him to help them solve math problems and were fascinated with his wooden clock. But they didn't become good friends with Ben.

Ben never married. Perhaps he didn't have time to look for a wife or maybe his life was full without a wife and children. Whatever the drawbacks to life along the Patapsco River, Ben seemed content. Then one day in 1771 a new family moved near Ben and his mother. It was the Ellicotts. Their coming would change Ben's life.

ANDREW ELLICOTT

Surveyor Andrew Ellicott and his brothers
came to Maryland to build a mill on the
Patapsco River, hoping to supply flour
and cornmeal to the city of Baltimore.
Ben became good friends with the Ellicotts.

3

New Neighbors

en's new neighbors arrived in 1771. The Ellicott family came from Pennsylvania to build
a mill on the Patapsco River. Three brothers came
first and later their families joined them. The Ellicott
brothers hoped to sell flour and cornmeal to the
people who lived nearby in a new city named Baltimore. At first the area farmers were puzzled. Where
would the mill get corn and wheat to grind? Farmers
near the Patapsco River grew mostly tobacco.

The Ellicott brothers had the answer. At first they
ground the grain they grew on their own land near
the mill. It didn't take long for the area farmers to
see that there was money to be made. Soon they

planted corn and wheat to have ground at the mill and sell in Baltimore.

Ellicott's Lower Mills took three years to build. The mill stood less than a mile from the Banneker farm. Ben watched as the stone building slowly went up. The Ellicotts had hired many workmen to help. It was a busy scene and very different from what Ben had been used to.

The workers needed food, but it was too far to go to Baltimore every day for supplies. The Ellicotts arranged with Ben and his mother for the Banneker farm to provide fresh vegetables and fruit and chicken to the workers. Mary Banneker was more than 70 years old, but she did a brisk business with the Ellicotts.

Ben's mother usually delivered the supplies, but Ben visited the mill whenever he could find the time. After a while the Ellicotts built a store. It was a good place to hear the latest news while picking up supplies. Ben wasn't used to so many people, but he soon found that he could talk easily with them. Before long Ben's

Ellicott's Lower Mills brought a lot of business to an area that was once quiet. The Ellicott store is the building toward the left with the second-story porch.

new friends at the store started giving him math puzzles to solve.

Ben especially liked the Ellicott brothers and their families. He admired the way they had come from Pennsylvania to work hard at building their mill.

The Ellicotts didn't own slaves. At that time it was much more expensive to hire workers than to buy slaves. But the Ellicotts didn't believe in slavery. They belonged to a church called the Society of Friends. The members were called Quakers. Quakers believed that all people should be treated equally.

The Ellicotts certainly treated Ben as an equal. Their respect for Ben fired up his love for learning again. At the store he read newspapers from Baltimore and other places. He liked to talk to other customers and the Ellicotts about local history and problems.

The Revolutionary War began shortly after the mill was finished. No battles were fought in Maryland. Free blacks like Ben didn't have to join the army. Ben's life stayed much the same during the great struggle for independence from England. Money was scarce during the war. That made it hard for the Ellicotts to keep the mill running. But at last the war was over. Business at the mill improved. The Ellicotts began to

The Ellicotts were Quakers, like this couple.
Quakers have always supported pacifism
and opposed slavery, believing that all
people deserve equal treatment.

build again. First they built a big stable and then a school. One of the brothers had already built another mill up the river. It was called Ellicott's Upper Mills.

During the war years Ben became friends with George Ellicott. George was the son of one of the brothers who started the mill. He was much younger than Ben. In spite of that difference, they became good friends.

George did many kinds of work for the Ellicott family. On his first big job he surveyed the land to build a road from the mill to Baltimore. George made maps that showed the best way for the road to go over the hills and through the creeks. After the maps were done, he told the workers where to clear the land.

Ben watched as the road was built and often talked to the young surveyor. Soon George and Ben began to talk about other things besides building the road. They found out that they were interested in many of the same subjects. George visited Ben in his cabin and loaned books to his

Even in colonial times, the harbor city of Baltimore was filled with activity and many buildings.

new friend. Several years went by and Ben was happy. He studied and talked to George when they had spare time from work.

George introduced Ben to a new subject. It was astronomy, the study of the stars and planets. George had bought books about astronomy and several **telescopes**. Looking at the stars became George's hobby.

After a while George found that he didn't have time for his hobby anymore. He loaded up his books and a telescope and took them to Ben's cabin. It was Ben's turn to study the stars. George even brought a sturdy wooden table for Ben to use as a desk.

Ben soon found that he loved astronomy. He read the books and taught himself how to use the telescope and some other tools that George had left. Soon Ben was working all day on the farm and staying up most of the night to look at the stars. He discovered that math was a big part of astronomy.

Astronomers back then spent much of their time figuring out the path that the stars and planets would take through the night sky. They **calculated** when the sun would rise and set each day. They estimated when there would be **eclipses** of the sun and moon. Together, these calculations were called an **ephemeris**. Sometimes an ephemeris was printed in an almanac.

Small paperback books called almanacs had been printed in the colonies since 1639. The ephemeris was the backbone of an almanac. It listed times for the moon's rising and setting as well as that of the sun. The movements of several other stars and planets were also listed. It was no easy task to calculate an ephemeris.

Ben decided to figure out his own ephemeris for 1791. He filled many pages with math calculations. He spent long hours at the telescope each night. A sleepy Ben got up each morning after a few hours of sleep. The cows and chickens didn't care if he wanted to look at the stars. They just wanted breakfast.

Ben's mother had died so now he had to cook and clean as well as do the farm work. It was a busy time for Ben.

At last Ben finished the ephemeris in the fall of 1790. There were 12 pages of numbers, one for each month of 1791. George was pleased and a little surprised that his friend could complete

Ben's skill in mathematics and astronomy helped him in the important survey work that was to come. He used Andrew Ellicott's equal-altitude telescope, shown here, to mark off boundaries.

such a difficult job. After all, Ben had taught himself almost everything he knew about astronomy.

Right away Ben sent his ephemeris to a printer in Baltimore. He wanted to see if it might be printed in an almanac. Ben contacted three different printers, but for one reason or another, none wanted to publish his ephemeris.

At the end of 1790 some men from an **abolitionist** organization became interested in helping Ben. But by then it was too late to get the almanac published for 1791. Ben was disappointed but determined to begin work right away on an ephemeris for 1792.

Then something happened that would take Ben on a great adventure. His calculations for a new almanac were delayed because there was other work to be done using his knowledge of astronomy.

WASHINGTON

George Washington, the country's first president, selected the site for the permanent national capital, which was named in his honor. Much planning was needed to build the new city.

The Big Adventure

President George Washington himself picked the **site** for a national capital for the new United States. Maryland and Virginia both gave land for the federal territory. The capital would sit beside the Potomac River. Up until this time the government moved from one city to another for many years. Now it was time to stay put.

The site was chosen. Next came a land survey. Many measurements are needed before a city can be planned. A surveyor makes those measurements. Major Andrew Ellicott IV, George's cousin, was chosen to be the surveyor. He asked George to be his main assistant, but George was too busy with his own work.

George told Andrew that he should ask Ben to be his assistant. The assistant would make many of the astronomical calculations needed for the survey. Ben's new skills in astronomy made him the perfect choice. Major Ellicott agreed about Ben's skills, but he worried about Ben's age. Ben was 59 years old. The work might be too hard for him.

At last George convinced his cousin to choose Ben. Ben agreed to take the job. In late January 1791 Major Ellicott arrived to visit his mother, who lived at the Upper Mills. From there Andrew and Ben would travel to the site for the new capital.

Ben quickly made plans for his trip. He was so excited that it was hard to concentrate on making arrangements. Ben had never been on a trip before. Excited or not, he had to get someone to take care of his cows and horses and chickens. His sisters lived nearby and agreed to look after the farm while he was gone.

Next Ben had to decide what to pack for his

trip. George's wife, Elizabeth, helped Ben pick out what clothes he must take. She knew that he might meet some important men while working on the survey. Ben was glad to have her help. He wanted to look his best.

At last Ben was ready to leave. He stopped by the Lower Mills to say good-bye to George. George was almost as excited as Ben. He felt happy that his good friend would be working on such an important job. They talked about the work and the fine instruments that Ben would be using. Andrew Ellicott owned some very expensive **surveying** instruments. Ben could hardly believe that he would be able to use them.

Ben and Major Ellicott set off on horseback. Ben probably felt sore by the time they reached Alexandria, Virginia, on February 7. He wasn't used to riding so far. While they waited for the rainy weather to stop, Major Ellicott bought equipment and hired workers. Ben walked through the streets. Alexandria was the biggest town he'd ever seen.

Everywhere he looked Ben saw soldiers and sailors and storekeepers. Ships unloaded their **cargoes** on the wharf by the harbor. Different languages echoed around him. A new world stretched out before Ben.

Finally the rain stopped. Major Ellicott and Ben and the workers traveled into the woods near Alexandria. Major Ellicott chose a site for the base camp. He put the camp on the highest point of the area. This would help make the calculations more accurate.

Ben and the other surveying team members cleared the ground, set up tents, and unloaded the instruments. At last they were ready to begin the survey.

Thomas Jefferson had given several instructions to Major Ellicott. Mr. Jefferson was Secretary of State at that time. According to those instructions, Ben and Major Ellicott were to lay out **boundary lines** for a 10-mile square. The capital city would be built within the larger federal territory.

In 1791 Ben was chosen to help survey the land for the country's new capital. He is seen here at work on the plans.

Ben's most important job was to tend to the astronomical clock. Surveyors looked at the stars at night to make measurements. These measurements were used in the daytime to help mark off straight boundary lines. Each time the surveyor looked at the stars, he wrote down the exact time as shown on the astronomical clock. The clock had to be very accurate.

Ben watched over the clock where it sat on a level tree stump. He had to wind it and make sure it didn't get too cold. If the clock got too cold, it might not keep the correct time. The clock and its stump base sat under a tent. Ben slept in the tent so he could keep a close eye on the delicate instrument.

Ben didn't get to sleep much. After staying awake to look at the stars, Ben had to stay awake longer to give his report to Major Ellicott. Next he had to make **observations** of the sun's position in the sky. Those observations helped him keep the clock running correctly. Often it was late afternoon before he could take a nap.

It was cold and wet in the observation tent. Sometimes Ben's bones ached, and he was

Astronomical clocks had to be extremely accurate so surveyors could record the exact time of their celestial observations. The clock Ben used was no doubt smaller than this elaborate one in France, but would have had to be just as accurate.

always tired. But he didn't mind. His job made up for any ache or pain. He loved to use each of the fine instruments. And he was learning new things every day. Ben might be almost 60 years old, but he still wanted to learn.

The survey work proceeded slowly but steadily. Spring weather arrived, which helped Ben's achy bones. When he had a few free moments, Ben began to calculate a new ephemeris. His work on the survey was improving his skills. Now it was much easier to figure out the tables. Even so it still needed more time than Ben had while working for Major Ellicott.

President George Washington visited the survey site on March 28, 1791. He stayed at Suter's Tavern in Georgetown. Major Ellicott met with the president to report the progress made. Ben may have met and talked to the president at that time as well.

By late April the first part of the survey had been finished. The four corners for the 10-mile square were marked. Major Ellicott's two brothers had arrived to help with the survey. Ben had to make a decision. Should he stay longer to work on the project? Or should he go home? He loved his new work, but he was tired. His sisters had been taking care of his farm for many weeks. Planting season had arrived. All of these reasons made Ben decide to go home.

There was one more reason. He still wanted to get an ephemeris printed. But first it had to be calculated. Ben packed up his gear and started for home. His big adventure was done, but he had learned many new skills. His next adventure was right around the corner.

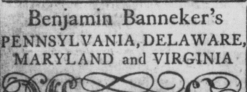

Benjamin Banneker's
PENNSYLVANIA, DELAWARE,
MARYLAND and VIRGINIA

Almanack

AND

EPHEMERIS,

FOR THE YEAR OF OUR LORD,

1 7 9 2 ;

Being BISSEXTILE, or LEAP-YEAR, and the SIX-
TEENTH YEAR of AMERICAN INDEPENDENCE,
which commenced *July* 4, 1776.

CONTAINING, the Motions of the Sun and Moon, the true
Places and Aspects of the Planets, the Rising and Setting of
the Sun, and the Rising, Setting and Southing; Place and Age
of the Moon, &c.—The Lunations, Conjunctions, Eclipses,
Judgment of the Weather, Festivals, and other remarkable
Days; Days for holding the Supreme and Circuit Courts of the
United States, as also the usual Courts in *Pennsylvania, Delaware, Maryland,* and *Virginia.*—Also, several useful Tables,
and valuable Receipts.—Various Selections from the Com-
monplace-Book of the *Kentucky Philosopher,* an *American Sage;*
with interesting and entertaining Essays, in Prose and Verse—
the whole comprising a greater, more pleasing, and useful Va-
riety, than any Work of the *Kind* and Price in *North America.*

BALTIMORE: Printed and Sold, Wholesale and Retail, by
WILLIAM GODDARD and JAMES ANGELL, at their Print-
ing-Office, in *Market-Street.*—Sold, also, by Mr. JOSEPH
CRUKSHANK, Printer, in *Market-Street,* and Mr. DANIEL
HUMPHREYS, Printer, in *South-Front-Street, Philadelphia;*
and by Messrs. HANSON and BOND, Printers, in *Alexandria.*

After several tries, Ben finally found a printer who wanted to publish his ephemeris in an almanac. William Goddard of Baltimore printed Ben's ephemeris for 1792.

The First Almanac

Ben was glad to be home. Soon he was back at work at his table. Once again he spent his nights looking at the sky through his telescope. Often he napped in the hot afternoons. Ben found it hard to concentrate on the farm chores. He had begun to think of astronomy as his life's work. The farm was necessary to provide food and a little cash. But it wasn't what he wanted to do with his time.

While working with Major Ellicott, Ben had learned how important it was to keep careful records of all observations and calculations. One of the first things he did after he got home was visit the Ellicott store. There he bought a book of blank pages. He planned to write down everything. The book was expensive, but Ben thought it was a good investment.

His new ephemeris came together quickly even though the math calculations needed to predict eclipses were long. It took almost 70 different math steps to figure out the time of an eclipse. Ben worked first on scratch paper. After he checked his math, he carefully copied the results into his new journal.

By June of 1791 Ben had finished his ephemeris. He sent a copy to a printer in Georgetown and delivered another copy to William Goddard, the Baltimore printer who had rejected the 1791 ephemeris. Then he waited.

An ephemeris was the most important part of an almanac but not the only part. Almanacs of the late 1700s included articles and stories and poems. Usually the printer provided those rather than the writer of the ephemeris. Sometimes almanacs contained letters. They also predicted the weather and told when to plant crops in the spring.

At this time it was common for the same book to be printed in several different cities. Most printers sold the books they published just in their own city. A writer might try to find more than one printer for his book. That way more people would read it.

That's why Ben sent his ephemeris to several printers. Finally Mr. Goddard said he wanted to print an almanac using Ben's ephemeris. He paid Ben a small price for his work. Ben was delighted. Now he would also try also to get his ephemeris published in Philadelphia. Philadelphia was an important city. He hoped that many people there would want to buy his almanac.

Philadelphia also had an active antislavery society. The men who had been interested in Ben's first ephemeris the year before lived in Philadelphia. Perhaps they would help him this year. Ben talked to George, who offered to write a letter to his brother Elias in Baltimore. Elias was a member of the Pennsylvania Society for the Abolition of Slavery. George thought that his brother might contact members in Philadelphia.

Elias was happy to help. He contacted printers and other society members. He wrote a letter to James Pemberton, who was president of
the Pennsylvania abolition society. Elias remind-
ed Mr. Pemberton that Ben had calculated an
ephemeris the year before.

Mr. Pemberton wrote back that he was eager
to help Ben find a printer. He asked that Ben
please send another copy of the ephemeris.
Meanwhile Ben got sick. He wasn't able to get
out of his bed. Making a copy took many long
hours since it had to be carefully done by hand.
How could Ben do it when he was so sick?

Perhaps Ben was about to feel better or perhaps the excitement cured him. Whatever the
case, Ben was able to get out of bed and copy
the ephemeris in a few days. George arranged
for the copy to be delivered to Mr. Pemberton
in Philadelphia.

Now there was another wait. Mr. Pemberton
sent the ephemeris to two different men to be

James Pemberton, president of the Pennsylvania Society for the Abolition of Slavery, helped Ben get his almanac published in Philadelphia.

checked. Ben's work passed the test easily. Next

Mr. Pemberton asked a well-known Philadelphia

printer, Joseph Crukshank, to look at Ben's work. Mr. Crukshank had published many books and pamphlets in support of blacks and abolition.

Ben was pleased that Mr. Crukshank was considering his work. But this brought up a question that bothered Ben. Was his ephemeris being considered because it was an accurate scientific work? Or was it because he was a free black? Abolitionists like Mr. Pemberton and Mr. Crukshank needed proof that, when given the same opportunities, blacks were just as capable as white people.

Ben was certainly proof of that. After all, Ben had taught himself astronomy and many other subjects. Most astronomers went to school for many years to learn what Ben had taught himself. There was no question about it. Ben was a good advertisement for his race.

Ben's Philadelphia printer, Joseph Crukshank, is best known for another book he published to help the abolition movement. In 1773 he published a book of poetry written by Phillis Wheatley. She had been brought to the colonies as a slave. Phillis Wheatley became famous as the first African-American poet.

Ben wanted to help other blacks in their struggle to get freedom. But he also wanted his work—not his color—to attract attention. In the end he decided that getting his ephemeris published was the most important thing.

Next Ben did something surprising. He wrote a letter to Thomas Jefferson in August of 1791. Along with the letter he sent a copy of his ephemeris. Secretary of State Jefferson was an important man in the new government. He also owned slaves. His writings had shown that he was sympathetic to the troubles of slaves but didn't think it was a good idea to get rid of slavery.

Ben wrote a long letter attacking slavery. He asked for Jefferson's help in getting rid of the idea that blacks weren't as smart as whites. He pointed out that America had been a slave to England before the American Revolution. It's not known if the letter was really Ben's idea. The abolitionists may have asked him to write the letter. They knew that Thomas Jefferson could help their cause if he wanted to.

As a political leader, secretary of state, and later as president, Thomas Jefferson had a tremendous impact on the nation's early history.

Ben probably didn't know firsthand about the cruelties of slavery. No doubt some of his neighbors owned one or two slaves. But his farm was far from the big plantations where hundreds of slaves lived. Ben's journal and letters seemed to show that he was a humble man and happy

Prominent antislavery activist Senator James McHenry of Maryland wrote an introduction for Ben's first almanac, published in December 1791.

with his life. Yet he must have read and heard the stories of slaves who were beaten and slaves who were sold away from their families.

Thomas Jefferson wrote back a few days after getting Ben's letter. Ben was thrilled to receive Jefferson's reply. The secretary of state wrote

Ben wrote a letter to Thomas Jefferson attacking slavery and urging him to help in letting people know that blacks were just as capable as whites.

that he also wished for life to be improved for slaves. He said that Ben's almanac was proof that blacks had talents equal to any other man. However, Jefferson stopped short of saying that slavery should be abolished.

Meanwhile, Mr. Crukshank wanted to publish Ben's almanac, too. Soon Ben would see his work in print in two different cities.

The first almanac went on sale in late December 1791. It had an introduction written by James McHenry. He was a Maryland senator. His introduction told about Ben's schooldays and his astronomical work. Senator McHenry wrote that Ben's life was new proof that the color of a person's skin didn't make him smart or dumb.

The first edition of Ben's almanac sold out quickly, and a second edition was printed. Ben still lived on his farm, but life there had changed. It wasn't as quiet as it had always been. Now people stopped by to visit the author. At age 60 Ben was famous.

Benjamin Banneker

Black Heritage USA 15c

For much of his life, not many people had heard of Benjamin Banneker, but in his later years he became quite well-known. In modern times he was honored with a postage stamp in recognition of his important accomplishments.

Success

Ben liked being an author. But the success of his almanac surprised him. He was even more surprised by the many people who came to visit him. Neighbors and travelers stopped by the small cabin to talk to Ben.

He enjoyed the visits. Visitors often asked to see his wooden clock. They also liked to see his wooden table. Ben was glad to show both.

The money he earned from the sale of his almanacs let him quit growing tobacco. Now he could just raise a small garden and take care of his beehives. He no longer had to work all day. He spent his nights doing what he loved best—looking at the stars. During the daytime he could spend much of his time working at his table. There, he calculated a new ephemeris for 1793.

Of course there was no problem finding a printer for the 1793 edition. Every printer wanted to publish the famous black astronomer's next almanac. The 1793 almanac included the letter Ben had written to Thomas Jefferson and the reply. This helped the almanac to sell even more copies than the year before. People all over the country talked about Benjamin Banneker and his almanacs.

Ben began the calculations for 1794 early in 1793. The printers wanted to get an early start. However, Ben got sick and had to stay in bed. He couldn't work on the new ephemeris from bed. May arrived before he was well enough to return to his table. But he finished in plenty of time. Several separate editions were published for 1794. The different editions had the same ephemeris but different covers and articles.

Sales of Ben's almanacs reached their highest

point with the 1794 editions. Ben was more comfortable with his success by now, but it still seemed unbelievable.

The 1795 almanac had a new feature. Several editions had a portrait of Ben on their covers. The portrait was a **woodcut** print. It may or may not have looked much like Ben. The woodcut showed a man who appeared a good deal younger than Ben would have been at this time.

Sales were still good in 1795 but less than the year before. Sales for the 1796 and 1797 almanacs went down, too. In fact the 1797 almanac was the last one published. Ben continued to calculate a yearly ephemeris for several more years but none of them were published.

Competition from other almanacs may have been one reason that Ben's almanacs lost sales. Every year more and more almanacs appeared. Another reason may have been that people lost interest in the antislavery movement. The movement was popular again years later but not in Ben's lifetime.

After a few years of almanacs, Ben's portrait appeared on the edition for 1795, although he would have been much older than his likeness in the picture.

No doubt Ben was disappointed that printing of his almanacs stopped, but he was happy to live quietly on his farm.

Problems did come up. He rented some of his land to neighbors. They farmed it along with their own. They didn't always pay the rent when it was due. Ben didn't like trying to collect the past-due rent. The problem got worse as the years passed. Finally some of the renters refused to pay at all. Then someone fired shots at Ben's house two different times. Once his house was robbed.

Ben decided to sell his land. He thought that the land was causing all the problems. He had sold some of it to the Ellicotts already. They made payments to him and let him keep living in his cabin. Now he sold the rest of the property that his family had owned for more than 60 years. He was sorry to sell but felt his life would be easier without worrying about the land.

Ben's life entered a new and peaceful time. Selling his property did seem to help. His days were much alike. If he wanted to, he stayed up all night looking at the stars through his telescope. Sometimes he wrapped himself in his cloak and lay on the ground outside to stare at the sky.

When morning came, Ben went to bed to sleep for a few hours. By afternoon he was awake and working around his cabin or barn. He pulled weeds from the garden and tended his orchard. He liked to watch his bees as they buzzed back and forth to their hives.

Sometimes he walked through the nearby woods and occasionally hunted small game. In the evenings he often played his violin and flute. He enjoyed all the things he did around his farm, but it was the coming of darkness that excited him. For that meant it was time again for the stars to make their twinkling appearance.

Ben made a couple of new friends in his later years. One was Susanna Mason. Mrs. Mason met Ben when she visited her cousin, Cassandra Ellicott, of nearby Lower Mills. Mrs. Mason

Ben enjoyed taking care of his many beehives. When he was young he had to learn how to tend the ones his father had started.

liked Ben. After her visit she sent him a friendly letter written in poem style.

At first Ben didn't answer. Probably he wasn't sure what to say. Then he got sick and was in bed for a long time. At last he wrote back to Mrs.

Ever since he was young, Ben had been eager to learn. His thirst for knowledge continued throughout his whole life.

Mason. He told her that he had often thought about her and thanked her for sending him the poem. After that Ben and Mrs. Mason wrote to each other until her death in 1805.

Ben's other new friend was a neighbor boy. His first name was never recorded, but he was known to be Jacob Hall's grandson. Jacob Hall was Ben's old friend from his school days. Jacob's grandson helped Ben with chores like milking the cow. Ben also found it difficult to walk as far as Ellicott's Lower Mills. The young boy did the shopping and picked up any mail. The pair sometimes shared a meal, which was usually salt pork and corn dumplings.

Ben slowed down in his last few years but was able to live alone. He kept to a regular routine that included a short daily walk. On October 9, 1806, Ben went out for his last walk. He met a friend and they stopped to visit. Ben felt ill and went home to lie down. He died soon after. He was just a month away from his 75th birthday.

Ben's family came right away. He had told them what to do after he died. They packed up his old table, his telescope, and his books on astronomy. To these things, they added his journal and another homemade booklet he had called his commonplace book. All of these things were taken to his old friend George Ellicott. After all, George had given him many of the instruments, books, and the table.

His two sisters were to have everything else. They took his Bible away that day. It was a good thing that they did because something odd happened at Ben's funeral two days later. Just as he was being buried nearby, Ben's cabin burst into flames. It burned to the ground. Nothing was saved. Even his wooden clock burned up.

The light from that fire faded quickly, but Ben's accomplishments shine a light that's still bright today—as bright as the light from his beloved stars.

GLOSSARY

abolitionist someone who worked to get rid of slavery

accurate exactly correct

boundary lines lines that separate one area of land from another

calculate to work out by using arithmetic

cargo the goods carried by a ship

deed legal paper that says who owns a piece of land

eclipse occurrence in which another heavenly body hides the sun, moon, or a planet

ephemeris a table that gives information about the sun, moon, and stars

indentured servant someone who works without pay to cover a debt

observation fact learned by watching carefully

site the location of something

surveying making measurements of land before building a road or town

telescope device that makes a distant object seem larger and closer

wharf the dock where ships tie up in a harbor or river

woodcut print made from a design cut in a block of wood

CHRONOLOGY

1731	Benjamin Banneker is born near Baltimore in the British colony of Maryland on November 9.
1737	Ben's family purchases a farm near his grandmother's farm.
1751–53	Builds a wooden clock.
1763	Buys his first book, a Bible.
1771	The Ellicott family moves near his farm to build a mill.
1775–83	The Revolutionary War is fought.
1778	Ben becomes good friends with a young neighbor, George Ellicott.
1788	Begins to study the stars after George lends him a telescope and books about astronomy.
1789	Calculates his first ephemeris.
1790	Submits his first ephemeris for publication; it is rejected.
1791	Helps survey the new national capital.
1792	First almanac published.
1797	Last almanac published.
1806	Dies at home on October 9.

COLONIAL TIME LINE

1607 Jamestown, Virginia, is settled by the English.

1620 Pilgrims on the *Mayflower* land at Plymouth, Massachusetts.

1623 The Dutch settle New Netherland, the colony that later becomes New York.

1630 Massachusetts Bay Colony is started.

1634 Maryland is settled as a Roman Catholic colony. Later Maryland becomes a safe place for people with different religious beliefs.

1636 Roger Williams is thrown out of the Massachusetts Bay Colony. He settles Rhode Island, the first colony to give people freedom of religion.

1682 William Penn forms the colony of Pennsylvania.

1688 Pennsylvania Quakers make the first formal protest against slavery.

1692 Trials for witchcraft are held in Salem, Massachusetts.

COLONIAL TIME LINE

1712 Slaves revolt in New York. Twenty-one blacks are killed as punishment.

1720 Major smallpox outbreak occurs in Boston. Cotton Mather and some doctors try a new treatment. Many people think the new treatment shouldn't be used.

1754 French and Indian War begins. It ends nine years later.

1761 Benjamin Banneker builds a wooden clock that keeps precise time.

1765 Britain passes the Stamp Act. Violent protests break out in the colonies. The Stamp Act is ended the next year.

1775 The battles of Lexington and Concord begin the American Revolution.

1776 Declaration of Independence is signed.

FURTHER READING

Clark, Margaret Goff. *Benjamin Banneker: Astronomer and Scientist*. Champaign, Ill: Garrard, 1971.

Conley, Kevin. *Benjamin Banneker: Scientist and Mathematician*. Philadelphia: Chelsea House, 1987.

Farris, Jeri. *What Are You Figuring Now? A Story about Benjamin Banneker*. Minneapolis: Carolrhoda Books, 1988.

Kent, Deborah. *African-Americans in the Thirteen Colonies*. Danbury, Conn: Children's Press, 1996.

Miles, Lisa, and Alastair Smith. *Astronomy and Space*. Tulsa: EDC Publishing, 1998.

Warner, John F. *Colonial American Home Life*. New York: Franklin Watts, 1993.

INDEX

INDEX

PICTURE CREDITS

ABOUT THE AUTHORS

Southwest Missouri writer **BONNIE HINMAN** has had five children's historical novels published, as well as many articles and short stories. She enjoys speaking at schools and reading all kinds of books. Mrs. Hinman lives with her husband, Bill, and son, Brad, in Joplin, Missouri, where her grown daughter, Beth, also resides.

Senior Consulting Editor **ARTHUR M. SCHLESINGER, JR.** is the leading American historian of our time. He won the Pulitzer Prize for his book *The Age of Jackson* (1945) and again for *A Thousand Days* (1965). This chronicle of the Kennedy Administration also won a National Book Award. He has written many other books including a multi-volume series, *The Age of Roosevelt*. Professor Schlesinger is the Albert Schweitzer Professor of the Humanities at the City University of New York, and has been involved in several other Chelsea House projects, including the REVOLUTIONARY WAR LEADERS biographies on the most prominent figures of early American history.